Worshipful Preaching

Worshipful Preaching

GERARD S. SLOYAN

FORTRESS PRESS   **PHILADELPHIA**

Library of Congress Cataloging in Publication Data

Sloyan, Gerard Stephen, 1919–
  Worshipful preaching.

  (Fortress resources for preaching)
  1. Preaching. 2. Bible—Homiletical use. 3. Bible—
Liturgical use. 4. Public worship. I. Title.
II. Series.
BV4211.2.S57 1984 251 83-48911
ISBN 0-8006-1781-9

K481J83   Printed in the United States of America   1–1781

Contents

1
The Purpose of Preaching

THE WORSHIP CONTEXT

To worship is to be in the presence of God in a posture of awe. The one we call God is beyond category and distinction, beyond personhood and sex, beyond the being of any creature that participates in Being. God is the love that moves the earth and fixes the farthest star. Worship is finding oneself in the constellation we call the creation and affirming one's place there.

What do people do when they assemble to worship? They seek out each other's company to acknowledge the Love that surrounds them, attracts them, impels them. If they live their lives regularly in the presence of the Holy and gather on Sunday to do the same in common, coming together in this way makes eminently good sense. If they do not live their lives in God's presence, regular assembly *may* lead to a posture of awe, but this is by no means assured.

The motives that bring people regularly to church are obscure, even to them. Their presence is already an act of faith, however feeble and inchoate. The question for the worship assembly—the leaders and the led—is this: what best use can be made of the time now that this handful, this half-filled building, this large crowded church is a reality? How shall we pray? Pastors and people are gathered in expectancy of prayer. Shall we do so in awe before the Most High who is at the same time more present to us than we are to ourselves?

Speech and Nonverbal Symbols

Nowadays all of us live in a highly verbal society. We are deluged with words. All-news radio blares out at us constantly, even at those who turn the switch spasmodically on the hour to get the "lead stories." The hard sell of advertisers on TV and radio is unrelenting. Sports figures have every least fumble, error, and breakaway play teased out of them by sportscasters in a never-ending replay. Disc jockeys, talk-show hosts, and commentators with and without wisdom go on endlessly. If our culture does not do much communicating it is hardly from lack of trying.

All this means that in the area of public worship nonverbal, symbolic language is in a favored position. Silence is literally golden if it is prepared for as an opportunity to commune with the Love that surrounds us. Even as a chance to explore our own so little-experienced selves it is a time of great importance. When it comes to such matters as sacramental rites, the bread and wine, oil and water, fire and ashes are able to speak our moods and convictions at the point where words fail us. We have heard all the religious arguments pro and con. We have nearly done ourselves to death with talking. The pass is reached at which symbolic speech can say for us what words cannot. We place ourselves before God and let mute, symbolic actions speak for us.

At this point two things occur. We discover our embarrassment at entering uninhibitedly into sacred rite, however at ease we are with secular rites. And we discover that we have no special talent for doing anything human wordlessly. Words, potentially always a rich resource, are in this case a sign of our poverty. We are ill at ease in doing anything conscious, not to say serious and sacred, without the help of words.

That is perfectly understandable. Whether in a "liturgical" tradition or not, all of us have grown up in a world where worship was talk. To praise God was to speak or sing. To thank God was to speak or sing. To petition God for our needs was to speak—in a litanic tradition to sing. There was throughout the worship act the substitution of sacred rhetoric for secular rhetoric, pious talk for everyday talk, one world of discourse for another.

Sameness and Newness in Liturgy

Now we hear new demands placed on us. We are counseled to "let the rite speak to us." We are invited by our service books to devise alternative rites. These rites are neither gimmicky interruptions of stipulated prayer forms nor shallow interpretations of an ancient behavior that possesses the weight of tradition. They are reflections on tradition that result in powerful adaptation or modification, however minute. Above all, the invitation offered in all the churches is to "get inside" our familiar religious behavior and let it become a new skin to us, an authentic human and communal way of being a people before God.

The challenge is not easy to respond to. In the first place, we tend to pray out of the service books that are provided for us. They are the work of centuries, edited lately by the learned and the pastoral of our own time, but they are not *our* work. These books came out of our common faith but they did not come out of our life experiences. They did not come out of us. Even those in the free church traditions that practice extemporaneous prayer have long ago settled into "orders of service" that are as fixed and familiar as any eucharistic order or communion service in a church committed to liturgical books. Our thoughts about God, our expression of thanks at God's deed in Christ tend to have assumed an iron form. Even pentecostal and charismatic believers have put the Holy Spirit on a certain regimen. We pray, all of us, as we have been programmed to pray.

This predictable rhythm is not an altogether bad thing.

The challenge of constant creativity would be beyond us. People are able to respond to the differences represented by a baptism or a wedding or a funeral because the life circumstances differ. No one needs to be nudged into grief or joy. The human reality experienced sees to that. Similarly, the Christmas mood and the Easter mood are self-defined in Christian assemblies that mark the times and seasons. Even those Christians who do not keep a calendar of feasts commemorate the mystery of salvation differently in summer and winter. These differences of occasion and season apart, however, we are none of us inventive enough to praise the Lord in a completely different way on this Sunday or that, in bleak February or golden May. There is a certain sameness to life that needs to be matched by sameness in the worship event.

It is good, therefore, that we fit comfortably into a familiar rhythm, a *liturgy* of Bible reading, and preaching, hymn-singing, and eucharistic prayer that helps us reassert our identity as a community of believers. Constant innovation and change would do little to upbuild us in walking the way that is Christ. It might even undo us. He is stable, firm, sure. Like the God and Father he leads us to, he changes not. The Spirit of God — who is none other than the Spirit of Christ — is fixed and firm. The Spirit leads us to an existence centered in God. The symbolic behavior we engage in at prayer must speak somehow to the reality of the Rock of Israel who is our refuge and our strength. Public prayer must have a certain fixed character or we will be set emotionally adrift in a life whose flux is more than most of us can bear.

Such is the case for stability and sameness. How, on the other hand, can the God of surprises be adequately testified to, the one who says "Behold, I make all things new"? For, in fact, that is who God is for those who view the creation with fresh eyes every day. What does an assembly of Christians do to witness to the life in them of a God who as Spirit is ever fresh and new? The "dead" or the alienated congregation testifies that it stopped participating in worship long ago. Why? Because what happens to it in church is always the same. There are no new insights as life progresses and the world changes. There is no awareness in the worship service of life's real problems, no relation between the worship in which we participate and life as it is lived.

Other, deeper reasons exist for widespread abstention from worship, but this is the one most often alleged. And it is valid.

There are for many people at least two worlds in Christian life, one our everyday reality and the other the reality called "church." The latter appeals to many for its unrealism, for the fact that it leaves the real world undisturbed. There are on the other hand some who cannot endure the one thing about worship behavior that recommends it so strongly to others: its total nonrelevance to all that happens on the other days of the week. Yet there are not two different human races. The two groups are members of the same race who live side by side. Often they are found intermingled in church, doing the same worship actions but thinking thoughts a universe apart. Often the division runs right through the individual worshiper.

PREACHING AS A PART OF WORSHIP

This book means to deal with the human activity known as preaching — more biblically put, with proclaiming the word of God. It can do that only if it has first dealt with the human situation in which preaching finds itself. That situation is one of worship: the acknowledging of the holiness of God and the passionate love borne to all creatures by a God of justice. Until preachers get that straight we will not be at ease in our office. Preachers are leaders in prayer. Our preaching is one of the several prayerful things we do in a context of worship. More accurately, preaching is part of the one, prayerful thing we do publicly.

This being so, the homily must above all be an integral part of the worship service. It is not "word"—rational discourse—in contrast to "sacrament"—symbolic, nonrational activity: the comprehensible providing the incomprehensible with interpretation or relief. Homilies, like liturgy generally, are reflections upon, expansions of, the biblical word. They are reasonable exercises because the word of God testified to in scripture is reasonable. The biblical word is not gibberish. It is not speech that transcends human categories, or oracular utterance that gives assurances no other speech can give. The biblical word is a record of the dialogue of believers with God, their report on all that deity has done for them and spoken to them and meant to them. The Bible is a people's speech to and about and with the God no human eye has seen. These holy books help us carry on a conversation with the one who is life and all to us.

The conversation at its best is lost in wonder. Besides praise there are other, equally valid topics: thanksgiving, questioning, petitioning, complaint, challenge. All these activities the Bible gives tongue to under the rubric "God says." For our speech about God is God's speech to us. The two are one. The homily is a continuation of the conversation. It is Spirit-invested but not, like the Bible, Spirit-inspired.

The practical consequences of this view of the homily are enormous. The homily cannot be allowed to "upstage" the biblical readings. It is subservient to them. Just as the primary purpose of proclaiming the scriptural word is prayerful, so is the homily an exercise in prayer. This makes it unctuous but not oleaginous. Nothing about the homily suggests that it be delivered in the familiar rhythmic tone known as clerical hortatory. The prayer that characterizes the homily is evocative rather than overt. It begins with a preacher who is humble before God. The tone may be strong, the confidence in the ability to do the task in hand unquestioned. A Uriah Heep obsequiousness or a bumbling manner contribute nothing to humility. Both can be proudly self-conscious. Humble preachers are aware of the burden placed on them by the assembly and the whole church. They know that it is heavy. They have responded with a struggle and prayer that taxes them to the utmost. "To work is to pray" — never does that mean more than in the pulpit, when chosen servants give evidence of their prayer by the labor that has gone into the task. The lazy servant is "worthless and unprofitable," in Jesus' words. Such a one will not shoulder the burden of hard work — studying, reflecting, and refining to produce a commentary on the biblical portions that is a prayer.

Once labored over, that homily has been badly conceived which stands apart from the totality of the service. When people say to a preacher at the church door, "Good homily," or "That was a powerful message," they should not be curbed in their generosity. They may be commenting indirectly on a lifetime's experiences of indifferent preaching. So be it. But when they say the same thing more than occasionally to the woman or man regularly in their pulpit, that is a bad sign. It can mean that the homily (probably in this case a sermon — a discourse not closely related to the biblical reading, as a true homily is by definition) has taken on a life of its own. By some kind of fission it has come apart from the parent body, the worship service. It stands alone in splendor or in shame as a good performance or a bad one.

Everyone profits by affirmation, especially the humble. Humble preachers will be the first to know, not necessarily that there was something wrong with the homily, but that it was distinguishable as the feature worth noting separately in the total work of the presider. And they will regret this. Presiders at liturgy are charged with orchestrating the whole

in their role as facilitators of prayer. Our function as preachers has an inescapable quality that distinguishes it. We are
the visible representatives of all the readers, ushers, choir
members, musicians, and other worshipers. Because most
people are authority oriented, they fail to seek out the lectors
or musicians who have acquitted themselves well. They
center instead on presiders and preachers as if it were *their*
service. Despite that fact, the preacher will know that the
homily has not consistently found its place in divine service
until worshipers are enthusiastic about the totality of the service. Compliments on the homily, however kindly meant,
can be danger signals that it has failed as prayer or injunction
to prayer. Such homilies are still "great performances."

THE BURDEN OF PREACHING

The fact that public worship is a single fabric places a
heavy burden on all the ministers of the assembly, starting
with preachers themselves as presiders. Reading publicly, for
example, is an elusive art. One hopes to live long enough to
experience the day when words are so mastered that nothing
seems read, when song flows so freely that no notes appear
studied.

"But that would take immense preparation!"

"Right."

We are strange creatures in our approach to a work we call
supremely important in our lives. We view God as being most
forgiving when it comes to our carelessness, our laziness in
worship.

"God knows I'm no golden-mouthed orator." "We're not
the Mormon Tabernacle Choir here." Taking refuge under
such weak dodges, we deal with each other in a highly
discourteous way. And because we cultivate our gifts so little
we risk serving God not at all. Trusting in a specious "sincerity" we end up thoroughly insincere.

Change the circumstances of a homily from an ordinary

Sunday to the funeral of a priest or minister; a choral festival with dignitaries present or even with paid admissions; anything held before the synod president or the bishop; even prayer with strangers present — and watch the tone of the service change. There are, of course, new dangers here. Then if ever the homily becomes less the handmaid of the biblical word and more a craven before the "occasion"; choral song, instrument, and dance tend to become detached from their moorings in prayer. The operation can hardly be called a success on such an occasion if the patient — Christian worship — dies.

Why is it so hard to "peak" in the service of God when we are serving one another? What depths of respect for each other's persons and ourselves must we not plumb before we give the "regular crowd" the best that is in us on the hottest day in summer — even including time concessions to the insufferable heat? When will the Catholics among us realize that no human company can "peak" six, eight, and ten times each Saturday and Sunday and, as a result, abandon the idol of convenience for the true God of community? What will it take to face the ingenuity and labor of setting a large company of disparate people at ease in their worship — starting with all the participants' coming together and confronting the task in hand? Only when they are at ease in the matter that brings them together can they successfully be put at unease by Jesus Christ and the gospel. For this is the preacher's task!

To sum up: preaching is an integral part of the worship act. One speaks in the assembly to facilitate the people's prayer.

PREACHING AND PRAYER

To be sure, there are different emphases in theologies of preaching. They are not so wide among those likely to read these lines, however, that old theological wars about the

relative efficacy of the word of God and the body of the Lord
in ensuring the divine presence must be recalled. Christian
people are no longer notably divided along those lines.
Rather, we have in common a level of preaching that fails to
inspire and a level of celebration that fails to move participants deeply. This tragic twofold fact requires our attending to our common problem as a worshiping people. We do
not pray well because we do not preach well. And we do not
preach well because we do not pray well. As soon as we begin
to do either of these seriously, the other will follow.

All Christian prayer is thanksgiving. This is true whether
the Lord's Supper is celebrated weekly or not, whether the
Greek-derived word *Eucharist* is used to describe it or not.
We assemble in a spirit of thanks for all that the Lord has
done for us. But we cannot know what to be thankful for on
this Sunday morning unless the word of God has stirred up in
us remembrance of the divine goodness. That is true whether
the gift of God be centuries old or a matter of the last few
days.

"Let us give thanks (make Eucharist) to the LORD our
God," say the classic calls to prayer of East and West. "It is
fitting and right to do so." Then follows a review of the
mighty deeds of God in human midst—sometimes beginning
with the creation, sometimes with Abraham's call, usually
with reference to the mystery commemorated in this day's
feast or season, and ending invariably in the canon
(anaphora) with the cross and resurrection. This recital with
which the central eucharistic prayer begins has a stately or
majestic, even a cosmic character that makes it transcend the
grimy adventures of everyday.

That is why the scriptures are first read out and com-
mented on: to situate us not in Ancient Israel, the shores of
Genesareth, or the diaspora of Paul but in the presence of
God in our own setting—where *we* are "before the Lord."
The central portion of any prayer, eucharistic or not, is a

thank-offering of bruised and contrite hearts. This can only follow on an assessment of how and where we are — "standing in the need of prayer." Such a review comes in the service of the word, Bible and homily together. It provides reasons why heart and voice must join in a prayer called Eucharist, thanksgiving. First, effective exploration of God's word without the opportunity to give thanks in symbolic act is a cruel abortment. Second, the call to such an act when our own lives have not been explored, only those of biblical prophets and apostles, is an exercise in religious imagination. The first says: You have examined all the reasons to express your thankfulness, but why bother? The second says: Be thankful blindly without considering in your hearts why. Neither position is satisfactory for a people that has accepted the challenge of addressing God through Christ in terms of affection and awe. In Zen you can hear the sound of one hand clapping. Christian hands are two. There is no effective word without sacrament, no effective sacrament without word.

The reality of congregational life must be put starkly. Without worshipful preaching that probes the depths of our human lives the people perish.

What a work that probing is in the community called church! A preacher should say: "I could die happy if I were to do a thing like that — prepare people to offer thanks to God *one time only*, break the loaf of God's word into fragments and share it just once!"

This book is intended as a dialogue between someone who preaches every Sunday and others who do the same. It invites preachers to that peculiar utopia of the servant called "preacher," to the homily that touches every heart — not every Sunday but *once*. Achieving this should make the effort of a lifetime worth the candle, helping us then to "bless God and die."

2
Preparation for Preaching

THE NEED FOR WORK

Preaching well is a great labor. That is the chief reason it does not happen very often. It requires too much of us.

If we are normal we prefer doing almost anything to preparing to preach. We put off our preparation so perilously close to the time of delivery that the homily's vigor is threatened by inadequate preparation time. Random reading, hospital visiting, works of social welfare, "doing the books" (conferring with the head of the finance committee) are more attractive options than facing blank sheets of paper with a blank mind.

Some sermons write themselves. A biblical homily never does. This is to say that an occasion or a happening will at times be so to the fore in the minds of people and preacher that the only problem is how to give it expression. A widely known and loved member of the community is taken swiftly from the people's midst; the industry in town that employs the most parishioners is threatened with closing; an officeholder or a piece of legislation represents a shocking betrayal of public trust, and the moral issues are clear.

These events that touch the lives of many call in question the goodness of Providence or threaten the existence of the body human. They require that then if ever the assembly act as committed Christians. Thoughts and words on such occasions tumble out in profusion. The problem here is one of restraint, lest the preacher immerse the hearer in a bath of indignation or emotion that has not sought its roots in the gospel. Apart from the church calendar there will be one, perhaps two days in the year when a sermon topic presents itself starkly and unequivocally. Such motivation cannot be provided from outside, no matter how enthusiastic for a cause a church superior or friendly bureaucrat may be (missions, Christian youth Sunday, world peace). The importance of these causes can be conveyed in brief and carefully considered remarks. They do not become the topic for an effective homily since they do not have an urgency about them that originates with preacher or people. Homilies that are *heard* grow out of concerns that are commonly held.

The Hazard of Fluency

The chief hazard to effective preaching is having a gift with words. Strong, silent types from whom words are wrung like so many drops of blood have the advantage here. Their need to get a thing straight in their heads before they presume to say it is the people's best assurance. The preacher who needs but a topic sentence to produce a paragraph is the enemy of the people. Who will stop this cascade, this flow of prose? It is inflated, like bad currency without a metal base. A homily, even the simplest, is always an argument. It tries to get the hearer from here to there in a series of steps. Expository discourse has its own logic. It cannot survive too many diversions — echos of reminders of reminders of echos. People who talk on like that we call garrulous, undisciplined. An occasional free associationist is interesting. But they are few and they never end up as preachers.

The bitterest complaint against pulpit practitioners is that they speak too long. This invariably means that they use more time than there are thoughts to match. Having said it once they say it again and again — each time less well. The familiar male slander against female prolixity has no place here. Women who preach regularly, few as they are, are still preparing their homilies scrupulously and not going on at too great length.

Taped transcripts of our public oral prose can be unnerving. In conversation we make all kinds of sense. There is economy, force, at times wit. Transfer us to the formal, and *unless every word has been thought out beforehand* we become wordy. If you can endure it, listen to a tape of yourself, recorded when you were prepared in a general way to preach. Had it ever occurred to you that you were such a frequent "apparent" person? That you were a master of the hopeless hendiadys—two words in place of one, destroying any power the first might have had? That you were a confirmed addict to "as it were," not to speak of "any way, shape, or form"? Tapes of our extemporaneous selves make us sound like caricatures. Unprepared, spontaneous speech makes filibuster artists of us all.

Why do people read poetry and prose a hundred or a thousand years after it was written? Because it was labored over in such anguish the day it was written. None of it was written in a day, of course. A lifetime went into it. But on the days of composition there was sweat, the rejection of draft after draft, the scrapping of the wrong word for the right word and the line or sentence that did not say it for the one that did.

"But that's artificial. My people know me too well for that. I am Smith (or Muehlheimer or Murawski) and that's that. If I give them Emily Dickinson or Thomas Merton, I'll die from the effort and they'll die from laughter. Those 'homiletic helps' kill me when they suggest I quote poetry I've never read and foreign movies I've never heard of."

You are right, of course, Smith (or M. and M.), but you are equally wrong. True, your listeners cannot endure an artificial Smith. But how they long for a Smith in the best Smith manner. There is a thoughtful, prayerful, cultivated you that lies deep. There is also a surface you that is immediately available. The latter your people can have at any time. To preach well is to go in search of the former and as you approach pulpit or lectern leave the latter behind. It is a mistake to think that the scattered self is authentic and the gathered self somehow less open and sincere. Sincerity has a way of making itself known in the earnest, honest, exhausted self that has gone through all the steps of knowing exactly what it means to say.

"But I would lose spontaneity that way."

They are dying of your spontaneity. Your lack of terminal facilities (as the old railroad schedules used to say) is driving them mad, your trying three and four ideas for size to see if, by happy accident, one of them fits. We are sincere in conversation in one way, in counseling and in passing judgment in other ways. To be sincere in a preacher's way is not to rattle on conversationally but to face the awful challenge of the medium that preaching is; then get down to work.

Writing It All Out

"I get it. You want me to preach with a manuscript propped up in front of me. Well, I tried that often enough when I first started, and I'm no good with a prepared text." Again, Sister Stephanie (or the Reverend Mr. Baxter), you are right and you are wrong. Some persons are totally inhibited by a manuscript — as much by the one they wrote two days ago as by one produced by someone else. You may be one of the people who are literally "no good" with a manuscript. We have all had teachers like that. Consulting the papers before them they were a chore to listen to. Set free from their class notes they came to life. "Why can't they throw their notes away," we used to wonder, "and just *say* it?" It is a strange but common human phenomenon that some intelligent people who devour print for a livelihood do not speak prepared material very well. Another inexplicable phenomenon is that the natural born actor who is not in the least bookish knows what to do with the words of Milton or Shakespeare. This latter group never bobbles a line. They always stress the right word—even if it is one they haven't a clue about. The first group drones on and on stumbling over the simplest prose of its own composition.

To know the group to which you belong is a great help. Whichever your group, to conclude that you should not prepare the full text of a homily is madness. If a script is your enemy, do not allow it to get near the pulpit. But if there never was a script, do not let yourself get near the pulpit.

Preachers who produce an outline only, which they develop on their feet, are perhaps the gospel's greatest enemy. With friends like these what need has Jesus of Satan and his legions, godless communism, or a trickle-down effect in the economy?

A third group probably exists. This must be acknowledged, in simple fairness. These are the people who write things out in their heads. I have never had a person like this among my acquaintances, but I know they exist. I had a schoolmate once, seminary through graduate school, who wrote a doctoral dissertation on a theological subject on legal-size pads without any strikeouts. It was good work. And I saw the autograph prose of St. Teresa once in a museum in the Carmel of Avila; having neither erasures nor insertions these may have been fair copies, but, knowing a little of the woman, I doubt it.

There is, in fact, a small and select company who work out slowly and laboriously beforehand what they want to say in writing, and then say it. These people are human word-processors. God has not created many of them. There may be a company, even smaller and more select, who think out in their heads over a long period of reflection what they wish to say and then say precisely that, neither more nor less. I have never known such people, but I shall not be so foolish as to say they do not exist. Of preachers who seem to acquit themselves well without having written it all out, I have known a good few. But in no case have I been assured that there never was a text. And being a skeptic who has done much public speaking and been subjected to more, I doubt it.

In the BBC film version of Nevil Shute's *A Town Like Alice*, Gordon Jackson plays a Scots solicitor who, when he is called on unexpectedly, gives an incomparable tribute to a newly married couple. I am sure the novelist worked over that speech long and hard. Someone assured me, though, when I raised the question, that a British legal person of earlier in this century was in fact so disciplined in the speaker's art that the incident could well have happened as the film depicted it. I am inclined to say doubtfully, along with all the Romance languages, "It is able to be."

In 1980 I heard Ramsey Clark, former United States attorney general, make a set of public remarks in defense of the symbolic action of "Plowshares 8," social activists who had destroyed a nuclear nose cone in a General Electric plant at King of Prussia, Pennsylvania. Mr. Clark had not a single note before him. He spoke as appositely to the occasion, it seemed to me, as Lincoln did with the pencilings he had made on an envelope the day before his address at Gettysburg. You may be of the Clark conviction (on the doubtful supposition that he had not written out his remarks). I would not count on it. Stay with the Lincoln people. We have his Gettysburg address only because he later provided it. As to whether he looked down at his notes on the occasion there is no record. I would compose an envelopeful of notes every time if that were my type (four hours? five hours work?), then speak at Lincoln length.

६ ८ ४ १९

If you are one of those mortals who can write out a homily in your head, by all means do so. Meanwhile, assure the rest of us that it takes just as much time to do it that way (or more?) as by the ordinary route of typewriter or ballpoint.

THE BIBLE AS RESOURCE

A greater challenge by far than the labor involved in producing a manuscript is the uncertainty expressed by the question, "What shall I preach on?" The gnawing doubt strikes equally those who derive readings from a lectionary and those who are free to choose their own texts. The latter sometimes ends in freely choosing no Bible portion at all, or at most in employing one so minimally that it is only a springboard for an idea independently conceived.

It is not a bad plan to preach about what is uppermost in your thoughts in the days immediately preceding your worship. This will ensure your own optimum interest in the matter—no small thing. Your thoughts may not, however, be particularly rich at a given time. A dry brain in a dry season is not confined to April, the cruelest month. There is always the possibility of your having nothing you particularly want to say on a given Sunday, of your being in a trough of the spirit at the only time in the week that allows for preparation. One might reasonably say, "In that case do not prepare. Forbear preaching and tell the people why." But the likelihood is that even though you may not feel able to provide a word from the Lord, they nonetheless feel strongly the need for it. The congregation's schedules are not yours. To have accepted the office of preacher is to have gone on others' schedules, not your own.

It is a bad week in a congregation's life when its preacher has given no thought whatever to the implications of the gospel of Jesus Christ. Let us assume that such was not the case. It was just one of those bone-wearying weeks eaten up by a deadly round of activism. All was somehow related to the gospel but none of it was memorable, none sublime. The details of parishioners' lives, however absorbing of your time, do not make good pulpit fare. This week there was a multiplication of duties — with meals and sleep and uninspiring television interspersed — of a kind that would have been threatened in interest by a laundry list. In times like these it is a relief to abandon what is uppermost in your mind for what is uppermost in the church's mind. It may be a miraculous healing from the life of Jesus and its paradigm from the Elijah-Elisha cycle. It may be Paul's scolding of Corinth or his warm commendation of Philippi, a blast from Amos or a cool breeze from Proverbs. Whatever it is, these are the thoughts that are being thought vertically over the centuries and horizontally around the globe in the churches that use lectionaries. You are not alone; you are part of a worldwide community of belief. The people you serve through preaching are not abandoned to your poor personal resources, nor you to theirs. The whole church lives a shared life with the lives of all Christians and all Jews, indeed all creatures having breath who ever lived on the earth. And lectionary preachers and those who worship with them are on a global rhythm that day.

Referring preachers to the Bible as a great resource strikes some of them as of no help whatever. They long to think with the church on this matter but have somehow never been able to. Bible study was an academic discipline in seminary days. It has represented defeat ever since. One suspects that among this large body of clergy there are no consistent readers of the Bible. They first came to know it in other circumstances than life circumstances, namely through limited selections in the liturgy and classroom study. They have returned to it again and again but always as study and *ad hoc* challenge. As the companion of their days and nights they do not know it.

No preacher should be told not to *study* the Bible, for it

will reveal many of its treasures in no other way. But all must be told to *read* the Bible early and often, if brief selections for a worship or preaching purpose are to have any meaning. In our next chapter we will be more specific about ways to turn the biblical books from potential enemy to friend. For now, it should suffice to say that the world of the Bible must be dwelt within; it cannot be successfully besieged from without. A succession of texts read aloud in public forum or read privately before they are read out publicly can be so many sealed up time capsules from the ancient world. They may never impinge on each other or on the reader's life. Thus viewed they become bizarre intrusions into the life of preacher and hearer alike. Or they are tales about visits of God from outer space. Either way the biblical pericopes will come at preacher and assembly with jarring and dissonant force, a totally odd prescription for the business of daily living.

The Bible is a book of stories. There are likewise legal prescriptions there, pieces of poetry, and written correspondence. But mostly there are stories that must be read, digested, and told as stories. Dealing with the Bible in any other way will negate its power.

BUILDING WORD POWER

A challenge comparable almost to that of knowing the Bible from within is that of having the words to say what you want to say. It is a frustration to have a great idea, one that you feel must be shared with other believers, and then experience the inability to convey it adequately. All your best efforts seem prosy. In your head the ideas soared, but with their commitment to paper they were grounded. If you permit yourself the slightest flight of fancy it comes out as a caricature of good writing. You know what you want to say but the words won't come.

Your problem may not be with vocabulary but with your

expository style. Everything you write comes out sounding like letters from a Japanese schoolboy. Reading isn't the problem. Half your life is spent with your eyes glued to print. Yet when it comes to writing, things don't jell.

What must preachers read if we are to say what we want to say and move anyone to action? Poetry, above all. Any time left over should be given to good fiction.

Why poetry? Because it says what cannot be said. It does so by allusion, comparison, contrariety. Poetry plays games with language for the most serious purposes. Preachers have to talk constantly about God, whom we have never seen, to people who are in no better condition than we are on that score. Poetry helps us do that best. Stories can help in the same way.

It is a mistake to read poetry with a view to quoting in our preaching. Worse still, our people may suffer the crowning indignity of having bad poetry read at them badly. In the midst of a homily it sounds like this:

"A Poem"

That is not what to do with poetry in the pulpit. Such reading can turn Blake into bumpity-bumpity or Francis Thompson into Edgar A. Guest. Ah, but to read poetry as personal delight, that is another matter. Then one does not "use it" so much as let it use you.

Buy anthologies, good ones. Keep a marker in the *Oxford Book of English (Irish, American) Verse*. Read Millay and Cummings and Padraic Pearse. Pick your favorites, discard mine. But let the poets speak to you and through you. Soon you will be speaking the way you wish to speak about God — even with the aid of reluctant lovers like Housman and Hardy. The wonderful thing about poetry is that it helps you know what to do and what not to do about prose.

KNOWING YOUR WORLD

A final challenge to the preacher is to know well the world you and your people live in, the only one God chose to save. Constant conversation outside the clerical arena is the best way to overcome ignorance on this score. Listening to or watching news broadcasts may help; reading news analyses in depth surely will help. But simply being a news junkie may provide you with only one or two reports repeated endlessly, a single catastrophe or crime of violence with the names changed. To be better informed one needs to read a good newspaper and at least one good journal of opinion. There are not many of these around. If you live in a region where none of the best ones are published, subscribe to one by mail, even if it reaches you a day or two late. You can skip the major stories by then and learn from the comment in depth what they mean.

One needs to be well aware of the movements of the prince of this world—how he operates with ease in church and in state. The religious press will not inform you much on the first count, nor the secular press on the second. So read an iconoclastic journal regularly, an image-smasher as regards all our treasured myths and illusions—in sports, in politics, in ecclesiastical life. The rubble has to be cleared from the building site if the human being, in family and society, is to be upbuilt there in the image of Christ.

Only the Holy Spirit can achieve this. A regular experience of the herculean task of cleaning out the stable is essential. After poetry, read good prose about the world you live in.

3
The Bible in Preaching

IMPOSING A PATTERN

Listening to radio evangelists is not a very interesting pastime for preachers, but it is instructive. The styles of these earnest gospelers differ, but they have more in common than the things that distinguish them. Most of these preachers are from nondogmatic traditions. Yet the first thing one notices about them is that they hold a set of dogmas about the Bible that does not come from the Bible and cannot even be teased from the Bible except by a hermeneutical high-wire act. Among these are the inspired character of every biblical word and phrase (2 Tim. 3:16 is about the Hebrew Bible); biblical inerrancy on all matters human in consequence of this verbal inspiration; the divine promise that living by these words and no other means will ensure salvation; and the perverse character of all those who, even though they may call themselves Christians, do not adhere to these first three propositions. The message proclaimed as that of the Bible, moreover, does not follow from its books so much as find itself imposed upon them by a doctrinal grid. This grid is a brand of eighteenth and nineteenth century Calvinism that would doubtless render the master of Paris and Geneva livid.

Radio preachers — we set aside the electronic church for now — also have some nondoctrinal features in common. They tend not to prepare in proportion to the time allotted them on the airwaves. They are repetitive to the point of boredom. They are likewise nonhistorical. Nothing that happens to the human race interests them except people's capacity to sin and repent, to suffer illness and confinement, and to keep those cards and letters coming. Radio evangelists tend to have little interest in the Jews as a people of history or in Jesus, his disciples, and Paul as persons to whom human things happened. From Adam or Abraham down to Timothy and Titus, all are cardboard figures whose walk-through parts contribute to the drama of the divine mercy and human salvation in the blood of Christ.

This analysis is not an exercise in ridicule. That would be cruel and unchristian. It is an attempt to learn, not from the "competition," but from others engaged in a parallel work.

The healers of television are a different group entirely. The Schullers and their school are another. And the school of Rex Humbard and Ernest Angely still a third.

Theological Presuppositions

What all these media evangelists have in common — and readers of these lines with them — is the practice of imposing shape on the biblical books. The evangelistic claim, however, is that they let the Bible deliver its message unhindered, without presuppositions of any sort. The claim is not true, of course, but then there is nothing in any way shameful about imposing shape upon the Bible. The covenanters of Qumrân imposed one pattern on it (consult the fragmented commentaries on Isaiah and Habakkuk), the rabbis another (consult the tractates of the Mishnah). Gnostics like Valentinus and Basilides found in the New Testament what they brought to it. So did church fathers like the Cappadocians and Augustine. Some of the Orthodox (or Catholic) fathers had the good grace to say what they were doing. When they spoke of a "rule of faith" (i.e., a norm or canon) they were referring to the Catholic stress they put on certain biblical themes. The thematic selection was determined by the high points in those scriptures most greatly appreciated by the church community. Modern differences among the Orthodox and the various Western church families are largely of the same order—representing divergent emphases on certain aspects of the large mosaic that was the faith of the New Testament churches.

The modern preacher in a Catholic or mainline Protestant church is the inheritor of a theological tradition. These traditions were sharply divergent as recently as World War I. They still possess a measure of their sixteenth-century vigor but have largely yielded to a reformed (restored, renewed) catholicity, thanks to their common approaches to and presuppositions for studying the Bible. The theological assumptions of readers of this book, as we said toward the end of chapter 1, are pretty much the same. That is not true in matters touching on the papacy and church polity nor on the authority of the church community in the ethics of sex and marriage; but these are almost the only exceptions. For the rest, understandings about the Bible and how it functions in the life of the church are largely the same.

The Lectionary

Private Bible reading is a fugitive in all the churches that have a relatively high theology of "church," and this is probably not accidental. The exception is to be found among those churches where adult Bible study is complementary to the Sunday worship service. This may involve only 15–20 percent of Protestants, however, and perhaps 2–3 percent of Catholics. There is nothing essential in the ecclesiology of either Catholics or church-oriented Protestants to hinder their familiarity with the scriptures. In fact, though, declining reading habits and declining churchgoing habits—plus the absence of a conviction that the Bible functions as an oracle—have joined to make modern Christians (like their Jewish counterparts) increasingly less a "people of the book." Much of this development has come about through preachers' mistaken effort to achieve relevance in the pulpit — a situation that resembles nothing so much as the cultivating of a plant's leaves and branches to the disregard of its roots.

Lectionary proclamation and its attendant preaching is one of the best developments in the life of the modern church. Catholics had been surviving for four centuries on the thin gruel of the unchanging annual readings ("epistle and gospel") of the Tridentine lectionary. This frequently provided the occasion for petty moralizing in a spirit quite different from the biblical spirit. Protestants had got away from their heritage to the point of total paradox: in many cases the Bible was not even read publicly. They provided, rather, a selection of texts which were announced beforehand but then not preached from. In both traditions, the Catholic more than the Protestant, the Hebrew Bible was a casualty. The good news preached by Jesus was subordinated to his works of power in aid of a theology of his person (Catholic) or his saving work (Protestant). The careers of the apostolic churches were either disregarded (Catholic) or rifled for their examples of the salvation of individuals (Protestant) rather than being seen for what they were — communities of faith nourished on the Bible of the Jews, communities which produced writings of their own as the fruits of their preaching. The New Testament record is primarily one of a living human community created by the Spirit of God, not by a book of words. In that community anything that could be established as a word of God spoken through patriarchs, prophets, and apostles was treasured as a breathing of the Spirit.

THE HEART OF THE TRADITION

Back to our radio evangelists. They must be credited with having the virtue of singlemindedness. But, like anything human, that virtue can be a mixed blessing. When it fixes on a single aspect of a rich and varied tradition, it tends to be a vice. When, however, the *heart* of a great tradition is in question — the central concern around which all else is organized — singlemindedness is a virtue. Preachers in any tradition are therefore wise to be reminded by their friends of radioland that no exposition of the Bible, indeed no single homily, can go free of gratitude to God for the deed done for us in Christ and made a gift to us by the power of the Spirit. This expression of thanks need not take the Pauline form exclusively, as it frequently does in the Protestant-derived tradition we have been speaking of. Acknowledgment of the deed and gift of God may be Lucan or Johannine; it may follow the soteriology of Hebrews or Revelation. All are different, yet all are one in their awareness that the words and deeds of Jesus and the apostolic preaching that interpreted them are central, and that adherence to them in faith is what gives life to the church, indeed to all Christians.

At this point two clear characteristics of radio evangelism assert themselves. This evangelism concentrates on God's deed in the cross almost to the exclusion of the teaching and the acts of Jesus. And it emphasizes the Holy Spirit as the one speaker to the human heart through the biblical books.

Voices of the One Spirit

For the media evangelists no expositor like a church community is needed. The Spirit achieves a homogeneity in the message that far outweighs any differences of outlook among the biblical authors. Pointing out the nuances and all but contradictions in the various theologies of the New Testament strikes the evangelical as the devil's work. The one Spirit of truth is the ultimate harmonizer, even eliminator, of differences. Therefore the four evangelists along with James and Jude, John of Patmos in Revelation and 2 and 3 John are fitted to the one Procrustean Pauline bed — which is Pauline in the widest sense inasmuch as the three pastoral epistles and Ephesians are considered its four posts.

The lectionary preacher—who tends to have received a biblical education in a post-Enlightenment tradition—is ill at ease in the face of this position, which holds that the Spirit "says it all" in an unequivocal way. The modern homilist needs to realize, however, how close the evangelical preacher is to the spirit of the church fathers—who themselves were closer to the early rabbis than we are in their view of Torah and the prophets, namely, as a timeless, undifferentiated whole. For the patristic age, Genesis, Jeremiah, John the evangelist, and Paul all spoke in the one Spirit, delivering the one message. This message was not nearly so narrow as that of contemporary radio evangelists. The fathers were historically critical in their own way, a way that is not the same as ours. They had a marvelous sweep of outlook. But in the matter of whether the one Spirit spoke with a single voice, delivering the one message of salvation, our evangelical contemporaries are very much in the spirit of the first five centuries.

Thematic Wholeness

Many a Protestant and Catholic pulpit preacher resembles radio colleagues in adopting a singleminded approach to the whole Bible. Unfortunately their singlemindedness is often wide of the New Testament mark. Some preachers are totally absorbed by the authority that resides in the church, others with the compassion of Jesus for the afflicted or with God's rigorous justice in the prophets and in Matthew. Some focus exclusively on Mary's intercessory office, others on the delicate balance in personal human relations where God has little or no part. The full-time pulpit ethicist (usually concerned with only one ethical question) and the full-time pulpit doctrinalist (usually absorbed in only one teaching or at most two) are quite different persons. Both are distinct from the deplorer of the decline and fall of practically everybody. Pulpits today are amply populated by people for whom King Charles's head keeps creeping into their memoirs; if they have to have a fixation, however, better for it to be the blood of the cross than any other. For the cross is at least identifiable as the great central reality in the life of the human race and the community of salvation. Around it, all that Christians say and think and do can be organized. But all other total absorptions, whatever their focus, come in time to have an eccentric quality. The richest biblical preaching is that which incorporates its hearers not into a single theme but into the *whole* life of the people Israel and Jesus Christ, which is the *whole* life of the church.

LECTIONARY READINGS

What exactly happens in the proclamation of the Bible in the Christian assembly? The community goes on record publicly that it means to live its life before God and the world in Christ Jesus. The Spirit achieves this but that does not make it any the less a public, human commitment. Thus the first component of biblical proclamation in the church is the person, teaching, and work of Jesus testified to in the gospels. This is why Matthew, Mark and Luke are read out in successive years with John ingeniously (and seasonally) interwoven.

Christian liturgy is the weekly celebration of new life in Christ. No single Lord's Day or feast bears any other burden. But from apostolic times it has been held that Jesus and God's work in him could not have taken place if it were not for the work that began with the call of the Jews in Abraham. Thus we have the second component in biblical proclamation. Preaching is a truncated exercise if it is not done in the context of the life of Jesus' own people Israel. The church has many times drifted close to the error of Marcion in regarding the Jewish revelation as of no consequence to Christians. It does so most notably by not acknowledging liturgically the never abrogated promise and call of Israel that has continued from the time of Jesus' resurrection onward. This silence is a terrifying near miss for the church, second in importance only to the church's failure over many centuries to read out the Law, the Prophets, and the Writings consistently in the assembly. The present lectionary settlement is welcome, but it is saddled with the age-old tradition of viewing the Hebrew Bible as nothing more than a "preparation for the gospel," without a life of its own. Perceptive preachers will know through their study how to overcome the hazardous invitation to anti-Jewishness implied by this featuring of a people whose existence at a certain point in history seems to end, but preachers need more help in this than their bishops and theologian teachers are providing them.

The third component in biblical proclamation is the wild card in the deck. Preachers preparing homilies can see how the gospel reading takes the lead and how the one from the Hebrew Bible is keyed to it. They are understandably not so keen for a second reading that goes its own way. "Semi-continuous" is the description of that much interrupted progress made through New Testament books other than the gospels. The continuity in question is not marked by the sequence of the epistles in the oldest codices (and modern Bibles). Instead, Paul's weightier letters are distributed over the three years. Certain epistles are so featured that material like 1 Timothy, Titus, and Revelation are driven to the periphery. The first is read on but three Sundays (common lectionary), Titus only on Christmas Day, and Revelation a total of eight times in three years.

Preachers experience considerable frustration with the composition of their lectionaries. This will evanesce in good part, though, as they explore the ingenuity that went into composing them, especially the successive refinements that mark each lectionary from the original Roman Catholic to the United Methodist. Current efforts to produce a truly common lectionary under the auspices of the Consultation on Common Texts (1983) may eventually eliminate certain shortcomings of the five Sunday lectionaries now in use.

LECTIONARY PREACHING

The best antidote to incomprehension is doubtless a firm grasp on the liturgical key. The one mystery proclaimed each Sunday and feast day is our incorporation into Christ as the church and as individuals in the church. No overarching rationale for the lectionary readings should be looked for other than this. The staple of each assembly is a gospel reading illumined by a biblical self-disclosure of God to Israel. Stronger than a grace note, but not a discordant one, is the tone struck by an intermediate piece of New Testament material. Its intermediate placement is a clear statement that Paul's gospel (or 1 Peter or Hebrews for that matter) is not *the* gospel. Jesus' proclamation alone is that. But when Paul and other apostolic-age luminaries write, they train a searchlight on the Jesus who is Lord and Christ. When the beam is especially strong, nothing forbids and everything suggests a homily derived from this source alone. But when the second reading merely contains good pastoral counsel, advice that immediately recommends itself upon hearing, it requires no more proclamation than a good reading.

Preaching on all three readings — even when they all contribute to a common theme, as on the major feasts — is normally an unwise pastoral decision. Looking for a correlation among the three readings on an ordinary Sunday is likewise time lost (although at times some correlation is to be found). But to have three scripture portions proclaimed *and then disregarded* is disastrous. It robs believers of their biblical patrimony—having first disclosed their preacher as spiritually impoverished.

The Central Mystery

Biblical preaching from a lectionary is simplicity itself once the key is known—the mystery of life in Christ, his life in this assembly. That mystery is examined weekly under the light shed on it by the Spirit illuminator. It may sound dull—doing the very same thing each time the assembly is gathered. The one vein is so rich, however, that many lifetimes cannot exhaust it. The biblical light cast upon this existence of a people is one. Yet it seems myriad because it is the story of this people's love affair with God over many years. The Christian Bible is by definition an unfinished book. Chapters are added upon chapters in the lives of believers until Jesus comes as Messiah in glory. But the tale cannot continue unless the earlier years are recalled, savored, rejoiced in. A people on pilgrimage must know where it has been if it is to know where it is going.

Information vs. Exhortation

The practical questions attending biblical preaching on the mystery of Christ and our incorporation into him are many. One basic one precedes all others. Should the preacher make the effort to discover the life setting of each biblical pericope proclaimed, insofar as this is possible, or should fairly immediate application be made to hearers' lives? The answer is, at one time the one, at another time the other. The second technique is familiar. It is the one adopted by most Bible study groups or cells of shared prayer and action. Without recourse to learned resources one *sees* what is written, *passes judgment* on the challenge this segment of the Bible poses, and after prayer *resolves to act*. The objection to biblical reflection that is not action-oriented is that it is mere study without issue; this lack of *praxis* is, of course, what the Marxists have against Christians and all believers — this endless reading, listening, talking, and failure to act. Yet in Bible matters a Christian response might be that to ponder in one's heart as Mary did the angel's message is already to act. It is the first step, the one that matters.

In any case, the preacher must decide those times when a direct move from the biblical page to the people's lives is indicated and when an application can be made only after certain background has been supplied. A homily is not a classroom lecture or a study session. It is meant to move to action — thanksgiving shortly to follow and the subsequent amendment of life. Preaching is primarily exhortation, it is not instruction. Often, however — so delicate is the motivating art — instruction provides the best exhortation and unadorned exhortation the worst. The preacher must decide what is appropriate in each instance.

It is an affront to people's desire to pray if ancient material, however sacred, read at them creates a large measure of incomprehension which nothing is ever done to remove. Worshipers do not need to know everything about a biblical passage. A glut of information can be as frustrating as an insufficiency. They at least need to have a clue as to why the church thought this selection could assist them in Christian living. Someone did think that; there is no confusion as to why in general the passage was chosen. But what does it mean in this place and time or indeed did it mean in its own time? The priestly blessing from Numbers 6 is proposed for the Octave of Christmas (the Solemnity of Mary). Why? Who were the Nicolaitans and what is the "second death"? Why will Shebna go out of office and Eliakim supplant him? Even the terribly keen who sense a relation between "the key of the house of David" and Matthew 16 have a right to know what the Shebna story is getting at.

The plain fact is that when the Bible is read out well it

creates an immediate interest in its contents. When it is read out in pedestrian fashion, not to say badly, no one cares what it says. Preachers who have been preceded by good readers create an immediate tension when they address none of the obvious questions posed by the readings: the who, what, when, why and where of it. Conversely, preachers can be regularly thwarted if their carefully prepared homilies are on texts that cannot even be heard by the assembly because they are read so poorly.

The Bible is a book of stories (together with some laws, some advice). When a story is read well it arouses interest. "Tell me of whom the prophet says this—himself or another?" Philip in response launched out with Isaiah 53 and ended with Jesus, and the result for his hearers was conversion, faith, and baptism. When the scriptures are explained well, something important happens.

This chapter ought to end with a general principle to cover all cases. How about this one?

There is no limit to the amount of Bible study preachers should engage in—privately, as well as with other preachers and other worshipers—*so that they will know what to leave out.*

If they are pedants or paraders of learning, preachers will never learn this. If wisdom is theirs—and wisdom is closely related to the pursuit of learning—they will read biblical commentary for an hour in order to write a single uncluttered paragraph. They will run down a seemingly unimportant question and report, not on the search, but on the one small finding that is essential.

The Bible is the preacher's enemy when little is done on a regular basis to unlock its contents. When much is done, little of what is done need be shared. An assembly does not have learning as its calling, and the little biblical learning that is shared will be wise.

4
Integrity in Preaching

WORSHIPFUL PREACHING

The homily is a commentary on, or better, an elaboration of the biblical message that has just been read out as part of the worship service. Its purpose is to situate the assembled community in the symbolic reenactment of the one sacrifice of Christ. The whole church thus situated, head and members, gives fitting thanks to God. The assembly is made up of believers who through their faith and baptism already *are* Christ and are now gathered to be Christ in a newly self-conscious way. Preacher and hearers together place themselves before God in an attitude of readiness to the Spirit's action. One speaks and the others listen to an exposition of what God has done among them lately.

This description of worship and homily is not pious talk about a churchful of people that never was. It is a sober description of what should be a regular Sunday occurrence. Whether the assembly be plebeian or patrician—day laborers, the educated, farm folk, executives, the urban poor—the people thus gathered (at times a diverse mixture) are here to engage in prayer. If they are invited to rote behavior, they will pray and sing and listen by rote. Some worship patterns inspire their participants to very little. Christian worship at its best will call the baptized to be what they are: the body of Christ at prayer under his headship.

For this, an infectious enthusiasm of faith is required in those whose task it is to preside. Long familiarity with the office can dampen their ardor. Poor health, depression, a myriad of things can dull enthusiasm for the event. Worship has a way of happening with grim regularity. In the lives of the clergy it can be grimmest of all. But if for several days now those with leadership roles — especially the musicians and preacher and readers — have been preparing to meet the people's expectations, the venture of corporate prayer will be lively and Spirit-filled. Neither bad weather, the week's setbacks, nor any other limitations (so we pray), can keep "us, your people and your ministers" from doing well what we are called to do.

The office of giving voice to the assembly can be a powerful one. It can galvanize the worshipers to act — first in this work of prayer and then in the service of those who need their help. The homilies that move preachers are their own work of preparation. The message prepared will come to the hearers as a fresh one if it has been lovingly labored over.

What is the power of a homily? Chiefly the force it derives from the Bible. This is true for two reasons which are not precisely in the same order. One reason has to do with the power of the Spirit that informs the homily. This power is presumably the greater as the homily is more faithful to the readings. The fidelity is one of spirit, though the letter of the Bible is surely the optimum vehicle for that spirit. The second reason is that the biblical word would be an interesting, attractive word even if it were not divinely authored. It speaks of worlds and of people who inhabit those worlds in a way that sets these people of earlier times and distant places outside of themselves into larger contexts. It also situates today's hearers in a community as old as the disciples of Jesus, indeed of the people Israel, from which place they can be in contact with the community of all humanity. This faith-filled people — this people who as Jew and gentile, according to Ephesians, are not two but one — does the deeds of faith. The Christian is invited to heed the call of the patriarchs and prophets, to pray with David and the psalmists, to question God like Job and give challenge like Qoheleth. The challenge is to follow Jesus like Simon and Andrew, enduring hardships like Paul and John of Patmos, to *be* the community of faith. To preach biblically is to do directly what Christian writings do at one remove. The church fathers can still move their readers in print as they once moved the hearers to whom they preached. So can the Christian poets from Lactantius through Dante to Donne. All gain their power as stirrers-up of faith from that word of scripture that is immediately available to the preacher.

PATCHWORK QUILT OR COAT WITHOUT SEAM?

The subtitle for this section asks a question that seems to require one answer: the reader must obviously plump for the seamless garment for which the soldiers diced. That garment, however, is spoken of here only figuratively — as was probably the case also in the gospels themselves. A patchwork, on the other hand, is not a garment to be rejected out of hand. Joseph's coat of many colors may have been precisely that. The point is that the basic choice in structuring a homily is between unity and diversity, and the choice is not easy. Multiplicity, variety, attention-getting and holding have their importance. So too do simplicity and coherence, going in one direction rather than several.

Unity with Diversity

The Bible talks about everything under the sun, yet really is concerned with only one thing — the "one thing necessary" spoken of by Jesus to the two sisters of Bethany in Luke 10:42. Worshipful preaching constitutes a call to that fidelity in peoplehood which culminates in loving service. That says it all, though it is perhaps too placid a statement of Jesus' challenge. Jesus asked for fidelity and service, the old virtues, in a radically new way. Responding to him required a break with the past—everyone's past. Scripture's dazzling variety in the two testaments says only this to the Christian. The genius of preaching biblically consists in achieving a Bible-like unity in variety, a variation that does not destroy the one theme. "Sell all you have and give to the poor, . . . and come, follow me" (Luke 18:22) is one expression of that theme. There are many like it.

The readings on this winter Sunday in Epiphany, let us say, are about the call of the disciples in John 1, then the call of the boy Samuel in 1 Samuel 3. Sandwiched between is Paul writing to the men of Corinth about abjuring their prostitutes if they mean to be one body with Christ (1 Corinthians 6). The lectionary fare is rich. If all three readings are developed it can be dizzying. One needs, on this Sunday, to speak about one thing, not two or three or twenty-three. Shall it be the call of God or "no turning back" or chastity in one's state or the guilelessness of Samuel and Nathaniel? It may be any of these or a dozen others like them. The ultimate "one thing necessary" is a sense of corporate life in Christ that longs to give thanks and praise.

The town has been sundered this week, let us suppose, by the widespread drug involvement that has come to light in the local high school. A piece of state legislation is impending on capital punishment or abortion or the rights of the poor. A local plant closing has been announced. Whatever the situation, no one in the area can speak of much else. Does this then become the subject of the homily? No. But living lives in Christ as they are affected by the current crisis does. Training the searchlight of the gospel on the human event is always in order. It is never in order to deal independently with the event about which something pious, however rooted in the gospel, must be said. There are many contexts—from grief to joy, from birth to death—for the one text, "to live is Christ."

Every preacher has been told in seminary training of the power of narrative. "Start with a story and illustrate as you go." There are pitfalls here. Our radio evangelists are helpful in highlighting the chief one. They take too long to tell the biblical tales. Any scriptural narrative has a tension that dare not be released if the story is to keep its force. Take the call of Samuel at Shiloh. The tale is repetitious, but it is not dull. A mastery of the previous two chapters of 1 Samuel is required to know what to leave out in telling it. Or again, repeating John's account of the disciples' discovery of Jesus—a marvel of compression—can destroy the original version. Storytelling, like telling jokes, is an art possessed by few. The only way to master it is to do it with discipline. This means an economy of words and a search for the right word. No story tells itself. A good story can carry the teller away. If it is too long in the telling, the listener will nod. At the end of a burdensome telling no hearer cares *what* is being illustrated.

The homily must somehow return at intervals to the portions of the readings chosen for comment. This can be done by quotation of the text or by recall through deft rephrasing. Alternating the two is helpful. The homily that selects a single text from one reading, then goes its independent way, is usually a flat failure. Riches were spread before the assembly in the three readings, but slim fare is selected for serving. No one who has heard the readings can miss the point that *either* nothing profitable was proclaimed *or* the homily proclaimed even more loudly that God's word said nothing to the preacher; how then can it say anything to the hearer?

What of an opening illustrative tale out of the people's lives (or out of the preacher's life if it is something the people also share), next a move toward the scriptural segments chosen for comment, and finally an application to the life situation decided upon? All of this can be marked by departures from the immediate—be it sacred or secular—to points of reference in the texts that underscore the points being made. The formula can hardly be faulted. There is one proviso. It may not become a fixed formula. What worked once or one Sunday in four cannot work all the time. That alone is well done which is not overdone.

Developing a Single Idea

A technique that tires the hearer is the multiplied anecdote or the biographical or sociological reference that proves to *be* the homily. The illustrations turn out to illustrate nothing but themselves. File-keeping homilists give sermons like this. It is in the tradition of Alvin Toffler and Vance Packard. By this device Norman Vincent Peale has kept congregations attentive for fifty years. Content quite apart, the net effect is to bring home a single point by tiring the mind. What sounds like variation is in fact sameness. Change ringing gives the pleasure of the peal, but the multiplied anecdote is the repetitive production of a single sound. The data provided prove to be one datum, the many anecdotes one anecdote. The (invariably moral) lesson taught is too slight to bear the burden of the treatment.

The basic principle here is that the powerful gospel truth must remain the dog and any material in aid of it the tail. When tail becomes dog, as it can very easily, the game is over. It may make sense to give this plumcake kind of a homily once a year but no more. The assembly's response will be, "That was great fun, wasn't it?" People can learn from great fun. But only once a year.

Some preachers arouse and keep interest by recourse to history—church history, world history, local history. If fascination with history is where most of their extra energies go, it is bound to come out in their preaching. Other preachers live in a sports world or are into the national scene. So be it. That is who they are and where they are. A preacher who never drew on a second major interest in life after the gospel would be strange indeed and ultimately the suppressor of authentic selfhood. There is only one set of references

assemblies normally cannot endure: that is, clerical life with
its narrow range of interests. "As we used to say in the seminary. . . ." "The distinguished nineteenth-century preacher,
R., was fond of remarking. . . ." "Canon L. of Exeter, toward the end of his long and distinguished career, said. . . ."
Assemblies find these recollections as gripping as a dentist's
report on life in dental school or a banker's report from the
boardroom. Such revelations from the life of the clergy do
little for the hearers beyond reminding them what unventi-
lated lives, but for the grace of God, they might themselves
be living.

A frenzied search for illustrations only tires the homilist. It
literally finishes the people. When a snatch of fine writing or
a recently culled clipping says what the pulpit person is trying to say, it all but seeks that person out. Sometimes it will
sit on a study desk for a month waiting to be used. The
preacher cannot say how. Patience is needed. To employ it
prematurely can destroy the urgency it was first thought to
have. The time will come.

One of the worst temptations we preachers undergo is the
thought that we are dull. We mean to be interesting "next
week" — unlike the last four weeks. Then comes preparation
time and all those pertinent references, all those scintillas of
insight get homogenized in a long familiar way. The homilist
is deflated. There will be nothing available in the pulpit this
week but the basic Ruth Jansen, M.Div., or the utterly
predictable Father Eastleigh. The people could do a lot
worse. Preachers who think themselves dull tend not to be.
And vice versa.

This glimpse at us plodding preparers is the place to praise
the careful development of a single idea in the community's
life. Careful treatment cannot be given to trivial matters.
People are dying of triviality. Seriousness about life's deepest
commitment comes as a relief. Seriousness is not heaviness or
dullness. It is taking at full strength the challenge that life

poses and accepting gratefully the divine assistance to meet it. Seriousness can be lighthearted and gay. Nothing about it can be mistaken for unseriousness. By contrast, preaching solemnly about things that do not matter is unserious. People pick up the difference immediately, regretful that nothing will change in the next fifteen minutes.

Religious platitudes are the chief sign of a lack of seriousness, stock phrases marched up the hill like the jolly Duke of York's ten thousand men and marched back down again. Catholic pulpit platitudes would shock, surprise, make shout with glee the purveyor of Protestant platitudes. Protestant platitudes would move to ridicule and mirth the Catholic platitudinarian. Catholic and Protestant sufferers would not be amused. They would learn to their dismay what they suspect is true: that each tradition has a storehouse of cliches on which the seminary student is nourished over a three- or four-year period. Congregants have concluded long ago that training in homiletics consists in mastering these conventions of speech. The same adjectives always joined with the same nouns, hosts of verbs and adverbs that do not occur in ordinary life, language as a screen to block out reality. Occasionally a visitor to the local church will preach in another pattern. That person is a visitor by definition, a wanderer who slipped into the ranks in error and probably will not persevere in the life of preaching.

Serious Exposition of a Theme

A serious homilist has been giving a lot of thought lately to the importance of baptism in Christian life. The incidents, the people that triggered these thoughts are usually far from earshot on the Sunday chosen for the exposition. They have contributed to the uneasy feeling, however, that the worshiper long baptized has not given much thought to this gateway to Christian life since the family's last child or grandchild came to the font. Baptism is a well-known rite of passage. One does not normally meditate on its significance in adult life. A familiar stock of ideas quickly comes into play whenever the word is mentioned.

The homiletic treatment of baptism will be basic and carefully thought out. Is the symbol operative today, or does the fact that it is a childhood memory, perhaps no memory at all, render it inoperative? How do the water and word of long ago relate to the word that is being preached at this moment? To the eucharistic meal that is about to be eaten? When did the church start baptizing infants — or do we know? Why are some churches so vehemently against this practice and others so much for it? Was Paul baptized? Were Peter, James, John? What was going on in the mysterious hundred-year period in the fourth and fifth centuries when the numerous church fathers born of pious parents deferred their baptisms until the age of thirty? And those exorcisms that remain even in the revised baptismal rites — are they a holdover from the days when people believed in demon possession of the newborn?

The treatment need not be exhaustive. It dare not be pedantic. It has to be in some measure researched. The research will above all take into account the Rite of Christian Initiation of Adults (RCIA) and its non-Roman counterparts. But a homily must always go on from here to there. The "there" is a renewed conviction in the hearers that they have passed through a holy door, come to life in the Spirit, been sanctified eternally in the name of the Father and of the Son and of the Holy Ghost. If they do not come to think anew of their own status as baptized, then all the erudition displayed is useless. The story about Anselm's baptism of Augustine so carefully dug out of the *Confessions*, that lovely snatch from a Hopkins poem will not mean a thing. Maybe no single illustration whatever will be employed. A number of theologies of the baptismal rite may be quietly exposed in order to help believers know the different ways the church has viewed this essential initiatory bath. The impugning of "water baptism" is terribly lively in those Christian circles where it is "Spirit" all the way. Have preachers heard the debate or are we far removed from the discussions our hearers are drawn into daily? Can we expound a great mystery of New Testament faith without polemic or sarcasm? Can we expound our own tradition of this sacrament without calling in question every other tradition? We must try to discover the answer to these questions. Yet, a lecture has no place in the pulpit; worship calls for a homily, a development of the scriptures. But nothing about the homily says it must be unintelligent. Everything says that a believing people is deeply moved by the careful exposition of a Christian theme.

People at prayer are in full flight from a week of television. They know the ads that "grab." Their children sing jingles by the dozens. People know when they are being "conned." On-the-scene reporters chirp at us nightly from Tel Aviv, Tobruk, and Topeka, ending their reports of catastrophe and carnage with a brisk signature indicating that their forty seconds are up. Prefabricated opinions are traded by prefabricated people. "Commentators" discourse at greater length but with no perceptible change in quality. Almost no one speaks to the people in thought-out fashion on matters of ultimate importance. The homilist has a free field.

THE BIBLE AND LIFE

On the Sunday after the plant closing, a preacher does not wisely delve into fourth-century baptismal practice in Milan. A great Lucan parable of compassion in the lectionary can derail all previous plans to continue a series on moral choice and conscience. To speak of homiletic options in this way suggests the possibility of letting life topics thought to be urgent govern the use that is made of the Bible. Normally that is not the sequence. Normally the Bible provides the lead in expounding aspects of the mystery of Christ. At times, though, the homilist is convinced that there is something that must be said, developed, argued. In such cases the biblical word can usually be discovered to have its say on the question. It should not be twisted or tortured. A medieval axiom says that a few words on a great matter are more important than many words on a slight matter. A biblical word is more powerful than all others. Normally it comes from the scriptures through the homily, but it can as easily come from the homily through the scriptures. When word and life are seen as one there is no problem.

The seamless garment of which we spoke a moment ago is only secondarily the fabric of a tightly woven homily. Its primary reference is rather to the unity of word and life. Structure must serve substance. Integrity is crucial for both. The seamlessness has to do not only with excellence of rhetoric but above all with excellence of life. I have heard homilies of surpassing beauty, more meditations than discourses, that came out with medicine-dropper slowness. I have also heard homilies marked by unity, coherence, and emphasis that had no power.

And Joseph's amazing technicolor dreamcoat — where does it fit in? Flashes of light, even brilliance, do no harm if they are controlled. All the colors of the spectrum are contained in pure light. The quick phrase that illumines makes memorable speech — if what is remembered is not the phrase itself but what the phrase said. An assembly will remember this: the preacher loved us enough to speak beautifully to us. What then *was* the beauty? Just this: The preacher believed every word that was said.

May the homily amuse, amaze? At times it should do both. Should it convince the listener that preachers inhabit the same world as people? At all times. That can never be out of order — unless the homilist is so impoverished as to require slang or coarseness to make a point. There is on the other hand a common kit of phrases out of business, sports, entertainment, and the arts that, if used offhandedly without lanterns attached, can give brief assurance that the homilist was assaulted by the same barrage as everyone else that week.

But people tend to know that anyway. What they are not so sure about is that we preachers who seem so alive and awake are at the same time as on guard for the Master's return as the people they keep reading about in the Book. Seamless coat or patchwork polychrome, the people can handle it structurally, stylistically. But if faith does not speak to faith substantively, they cannot handle that.

They may keep on coming to church. But that may be the greatest tragedy of all: to be corroded by words that do not speak *the* word, by a message that says — nothing.

5
Preaching for Action

IMPROVING COMMUNICATION

Preaching is done best by those with an aptitude for it. Serving an assembly in other capacities — as people's counselor or comforter, the administrator of their property, the advocate in their voicelessness — is the best preparation for breaking the bread of the word with them. To preach is to console but also to judge, to teach but also to reveal one's need. It is, in brief, a means of communicating in which preacher and assembly speak and are spoken to. The enforced silence of the worshipers makes communication difficult for both parties. Everyone concerned has to work at that.

Theological preparation, usually culminating in ordination, certifies a person as apt for the work of preaching. That could have been adequate when received. Some preachers had an academic training, though, which even at that time was inferior. In other cases the preacher, although certified, never became skilled, yet continued to preach as part of a total ministry. The most usual cases are still two — the person of limited gifts who, through earnest application over the years, grows constantly better at delivering a homily, and the person who, having lost all interest in the task, preaches ineffectively. No one who does not try to pray can preach well. But no one who respects the religious needs of an assembly can preach badly. Homilists who love their people, yet find themselves ill at ease in the office of homilist, can sometimes arrange for their people to hear better preaching than they themselves can provide.

Since the homily is an integral part of a worship service, not a piece of learned discourse, the best thing an ordained person can do is try to make progress in presiding at that public prayer which is the liturgy. This means progress, too, in the deliverance of the homily which is part of the liturgy. Those who are tired of the work should cease doing it. This is a true counsel but easier to give than to take when ministry is all a person knows.

Yet the continued activity of preachers who lack conviction is a threat to the people's faith as well as to their own. Many a minister or priest continues to be enthusiastic for other aspects of the ministry than this one. The obvious solution to the church's unrealistic vote of confidence in universal clergy competence is to have the clergy do what they do well but not to insist (to insist that they not?) continue doing what they do badly. An almost untried alternative is actively to help preachers preach better and actually to give them their first taste of achievement in the art — sometimes after thirty years.

THE WORD AND THE DEED

A homily is a commentary on readings from the Bible that is calculated to move the hearers to action. The immediate action is prayer within the context of this particular celebration (whether eucharistic or not). The less proximate action is conversion of life, growth in holiness, service of God and neighbor. The homily has failed if it does not move the hearer to both the immediate action and the subsequent action.

The Importance of Being Heard

To do so it must be heard and understood. It must be recognized as inviting to a course of action. Inadequate preparation or dull delivery will not accomplish this. But there is more. Hearers so angered or alienated by the message that they feel a strong call to do the opposite have not been effectively addressed. Or perhaps they have: we preachers sometimes "get to" our hearers when we present the implications of the gospel. It could even be said that we "lose" them — but we at least have the satisfaction of knowing we have done our job.

Much commoner is the "homily" that is a harangue. A scolding well deserved is a scolding well delivered. But the pulpit hears few of those. Too often it entertains emotional treatment of matters that mean much to the preacher but little to the hearer. The gap between the two results in a torrent of words that angers or annoys but does not move.

Talking Their Language

But the most common nonmotivating homily is not of this kind. It is earnest. It may even be prepared. It is delivered in "Religionspeak," the tongue of a land with no known inhabitants.

That description needs to be corrected. The people who speak and understand this tongue (even without hearing it, so remarkable is it as a medium) come once a week from a country where an entirely different tongue is spoken. They are addressed in Religionspeak in a land called "church." No action follows from the nonconversations conducted in this tongue. They do not summon to action. Their subject matter is a practice or a piety in which the preachers themselves no longer engage — though they might have once — or the discussion of living faith in a long-dead language. It may also be the approbation of something about which neither speaker nor listener really cares — the local religious press, a rally in a distant city, a contribution to a cause the worth of which is assumed but never made clear. All this is a familiar phenomenon. Mention of it should not arise in a discussion of preaching. Yet it is the bad currency of an ecclesiastical

Gresham's Law that drives the good off the market. Every Christian knows this Religionspeak and recognizes it as the devil's handiwork, though the truth of this proposition is oftentimes hidden from the preacher.

This may be too heavy a charge to lay at the door of the very preachers who are reading these lines — which are intended to say something helpful to the faithful servant who earnestly wants to preach God's word but is unconsciously too wedded to Religionspeak to do so. "How displeasing this is to our blessed Lord and Savior Jesus Christ." "For which cause the Scripture describes them marked of God on the forehead, whom his mercy has undertaken to keep from final confusion and shame." "May Almighty God bestow on these good people his choicest graces and blessings." "Bowed low before God in sumble hupplication. . . ."

God speaks to people in their own languages. The language of divine service is very much one of their languages. Religionspeak is no one's language. It is conceived in falsity and begotten in deceit — both of which may be unwitting. The deceit is pious, which makes it worse. Only one tongue befits the word of God, the language of truth. People speak the truth in their everyday speech because they have no other tongue to speak it in. They manufacture another speech only for occasions — all of which share to some degree in falsity.

People also lie in their everyday speech, which is the language of sin as well as of righteousness. This is another reason why preachers must communicate in the language of the people.

Believers must know, if they are to heed the preacher, that their spiritual guides have some experience of life, that what the preacher thinks are virtue and vice are the same things they themselves call virtue and vice. The best assurance of this is the preacher's mastery of the language people use to speak about everything under the sun. Faith is either the stuff of ordinary life or it is a false view of everything. Religion as a compartment of life, a decoration to lend it tone, is a luxury no one can afford. Not even God would want to get mixed up in a thing like that.

THE DIALOGICAL CHARACTER OF PREACHING

If a homily is to motivate to a course of action — and it has no other purpose — it cannot preempt the hearer's part in the exchange. The hearer is a potential doer of the word or the attempt at communication is vain. But everyone shortly loses interest in a conversation that is a monologue.

Homilies have to have a large measure of dialogue built in or they die. Informing people about anything runs a great risk. There is an imbalance about it from the start which can get progressively worse. The homilist knows certain matters or possesses certain convictions that the hearer may not. Any indication that this is a perfectly fitting state of affairs can mean that communication is over. The knower who patronizes about knowledge possessed teaches no one. Preachers may know no electronics or very little about the national sports scene, but they do know a good deal about the Bible, church history, and theology. Worshipers expect that, so there is no problem. The delicate question is, when does preachers' knowledge or conviction stop being their possession and start becoming their burden? The answer may be that what is the preacher's possession need not burden the hearer, not after fourteen minutes or even an hour. Conversely, an intolerable weight can be imposed on the hearers as early as an opening sentence or paragraph. Jesus had something to say about heavy and insupportable burdens. No hearer should experience the gospel as a burden.

Caring About Hearers

Manner means much in an exchange like this. The simplest person can take in a surprising amount of new material and welcome it. The determining factor is whether the speaker really cares about the hearers and especially about whether they actually hear. Such care is the very condition of hearing. It is conveyed in the turn of phrase, the tone of voice. Jesus shared the profoundest insights with the simplest people. He had unlimited confidence in the people's ability to absorb them. They picked this up — and kept on listening.

Vocabulary can be a barrier to understanding. Illogic is a greater one. Good will is of no help when you are asked to follow a fuzzy argument. The greatest off-putter of all is the manner, not the matter, of the expositor, the strong implication that the preacher has precisely what the assembly needs. In every phrase it is implied, "I'll go slowly and repeat frequently so that you get it." But people are not stupid. When those are the terms, they neither want it nor need it.

Leaving Room for Response

A homily has to leave room for hearer response. If a story is told, people must want to tell another to match it. As in a good conversation anecdotes should elicit anecdotes in the hearers' heads. If an argument is developed or a case made, the steps must be such that the listener needs to follow attentively so as not to miss a step. The whole point is that the preacher is leading people in the assembly somewhere, namely, to a state of conviction that is their own. The moment they think they are being manipulated, "worked," their interest drops to zero. At that point they know that the preacher does not respect them but is selling them something. It may be salvation, the highest good imaginable. But they have enough sense to dig in their heels and refuse to buy. The terms are not good. The gospel is being perverted.

Every good homily is incomplete. It need not cultivate the sudden dramatic ending, the fiercely delivered challenge. A good homily engages hearers to the point where they work at the problem posed. They consider the options offered, accepting some and rejecting others. Nothing is cut and dried. A miniplay has been produced, and they have been offered a part. A short story has been told which leaves them wondering about the outcome. They have been helped to identify the importance of the things discussed with them.

When the homily settles every question it raises, there is nothing left to care about. The one thing an exploration of the gospel *cannot* be is predictable. That is the genius of the great tales in the Bible and of the parables of Jesus. They could have gone either way. A Tamar, a David or a Jeremiah, a rich man with a Lazarus at his gate did not have to choose as they did. There were problematic elements in their options and in what they made of them. When a story is told well, the attentive hearer pays it the supreme compliment: It could have gone otherwise.

ATTENDING TO SOCIAL QUESTIONS

The choices to which the homily invites are of two kinds—individual and social. The first type can be a snug harbor, confirming the worshiper's conviction that religion is indeed a private affair and that God is interested in three things only: sex, uncharitable behavior, and giving good example. Attention to social behavior can be unsettling. It is barely distinguishable from the political—policies in place and officeholders in power. It may even touch on parties and administrations. All this is a minefield. Better to stay with morally indisputable questions like the scandalizing of little ones or the destruction of a fetus.

The Place of Moral Argument

Indeed the above two specific moral offenses are not unimportant. Jesus spoke strongly about the first. His probable position on the second can be intelligently argued. The point is that *everything* calculated to lead hearers to a decision must be argued. There are unassailable axioms in human behavior, and at the same time there are no axioms. An axiom by definition cannot be proved (e.g., the good must be done, the evil avoided; more specifically, the defenseless old may not be bludgeoned). But an exposition is possible and even necessary as to why anyone thinks axioms axiomatic. When it comes to the arguable applications of these great, simple truths, nothing will do but honest attempts to persuade.

The assumption on which all that immediately follows is based is that the liturgy is a prayerful setting in which to make moral choices. Moral here means human, hence not always ethical but sometimes broader than ethical. A Protestant preacher may think it important to speak on the fate of the dead and to do so differently from the traditional view of his congregants. A Catholic preacher may wish to refine the hearers' convictions about the impenetrable mystery of grace and free will. These are theoretical questions about the relation of God to humanity. They have a history in the respective traditions as indeed in all of human life. They need to be examined publicly not as an exercise in contemplation but with a view to action. Jesus knew the primacy of the deed long before Karl Marx discovered it in a context of Christian disregard of Jesus as teacher. Calls to action in homilies are always in order, always moral, often ethical. The cornerstone of Christian ethos is a free and conscious stance before God in awe.

Individual and Society

Back to the individual and the social character of human choices. Like a horse and carriage, you can't have one without the other. The choices made by persons (or their inability to make them) are always influenced and sometimes determined by society. This needs to be recorded. Society's choices, conversely, are impossible without the determinations of myriad individuals.

The contemporary Christian in the pew is frequently overcome by the narrow range of choices known to the preacher. There can be an unvoiced anger over the fact that the preacher knows so little of life, or anger at what seems like easy party-line opposition to some of the few free choices that exist. Unless the homily somehow gets inside the personal struggle people are experiencing it cannot move to action. Preachers must give evidence of knowing the struggle at first hand and knowing the community support available — or lack of support — for taking a Christian position. People cannot fight a battle alone. They have to know that the whole church is with them, and not just by way of talk.

Preaching in the Robbers' Den

Take a simple case. Most Sunday congregations number a fair sprinkling of thieves. At one level they are asking for payment in cash so that no record will exist for tax purposes. At another, large checks are being received for illicit services or for no services rendered at all. The rationale for this behavior was arrived at long ago. No preacher has ever identified it to some parishioners for what it is: theft. Most assume it's simply a matter of business. Heading the list of such thieves is the cheater who passes the time at work with studied inefficiency and takes full pay. Employees who furnish their homes, workbenches, or kitchens from plant or store come a little lower down — but not much — on the list. The problem at the higher income levels is different and sometimes harder to identify; here the thieves pay off mortgages on $350,000 homes.

Pastoral ministers who preach honestly on dishonesty need to guard against presuming on a factual knowledge we do not possess. We must worry about committed information given in confidence. We know that indulging in clever innuendo helps no one. But there it is: the delicate problem of bringing alive in the worshipers' consciousness the Mosaic commandment, the counsels of the Jewish sages, the stern teaching of Jesus about defrauding others and living by what is not yours. Effective homilies on this subject — like effective homilies on anything — are written with the homilist's blood.

The basic stance is Pauline: the offense against the whole body of Christ by the sin of some members is a real problem. The church's thieves make mockery of its claim to holiness. The church is a den of robbers. The subject has to be addressed. Whether head-on or by careful crablike steps is for the preacher to decide. The first step is to be sure that *preachers* take nothing for nothing, having no truck with the notion "It's for the church" as a way to beat everyone from florists to the state revenue service.

Preaching on Public Morality

Is there any sense to getting at those who are absent through those present? Probably not. Vicarious targets are too easy. Besides, they give everyone seated in the church the comforting feeling that all sinners flourish at a distance. Pulpit "pro-lifers" can thump far-off legislators or Supreme Court justices as a substitute for facing the fact that our own congregants are probably the least respectful of the lives of the poor, and our own religionists the chief clients of local abortion services. It is easy to belabor distant governments for the infringement of human rights with never a peep about comparable infringements in the life of the church. The public moralist bears a heavy burden of consistency. Jesus was death on the hypocrite, public or private. The preacher treads a perilous path.

The path is that of the persuader, not the thumper. The first step is convincing anyone that the message comes from God in Christ and is not a mere human tradition. Homilies that do not derive from the scriptures are a sure way to put the matter in doubt. In certain areas of ethics, establishing a firm base in tradition is not easy. It requires hard scrutiny of the gospel, the Hebrew Bible, and the long tradition of the church. Questions of social and distributive justice are a notorious example of the difficulties involved. People guard fiercely their possessions and what they perceive as their rights. The political theory and the party voting line they adopt is sacrosanct to them — not to be touched by "church interference." People of means take a hard line on the alienation of their property for the public good. They claim infringement of their rights whenever a tax bite touches them deeply. The sins of corporations and governments are fair game for most people except the people whom these structures protect. The public becomes private and vice versa with alarming swiftness, usually through circumstance and seldom by a consistent process.

All questions of public morality are *ipso facto* political questions. No homilist can be innocent enough to think that there is an area of pure morality. There is no such thing. Even individual choices have immediate social consequences, and the social is the political. The assurance that pulpit discussion of the political can always be nonpartisan would be comforting. It is not so. Decisions are made by persons and by parties that have names — people who do not tread "the straight and narrow path between good and evil," hard as they may try. Neither can the homilist, who must at times describe public policy or fence straddling for the injustice that it is.

Defense spending, that glorious euphemism, needs to be defined as the international scramble for the arms market that it is. Hunger in the local municipality and world hunger must be spoken of in their causes and not just in their effects. It does no harm to arouse sympathy for victims far and near, but this can be frustrating all around. If blame can be identified it must be assigned. Above all, the measure of the assembly's complicity in a corporate evil, the complicity of preacher and hearer alike, must be estimated. A reasonable rectification must be proposed. Often the sole realistic effect a homily can achieve is the raising of consciousness on the enormity of an evil. It can propose small steps, the taking or omission of which will highlight the sore. Personal and immediate charity is always in order. Highlighting what justice consists in, as part of improved social organization, is far better.

Does one avoid the specific, the accusatory, the unquestionably partisan in the pulpit? There is no direct answer to that question. One explores human questions in all the depth one is capable of—not as a political scientist or economist or practicing politician, none of which the preacher is, but in the light of the gospel. The homilist is a public moralist and in that role a public servant. Christian people are starved for a gospel view of questions public and private on which they must make decisions daily. They suspect that Jesus Christ is the wisdom they need, but in a certain peak of confusion they do not want "the church" to have anything to say about these questions. The silent pulpit contributed to this contradictory formula so cherished by the American heart. Only the voice of Christ and the church, meaning all his people, as one voice and not two, can dispel it. This will happen when the message is actively received and thereby *becomes* the word of the church.

6
Preaching Life

THE REWARDS OF PREACHING
Is there any reward?
I'm beginning to doubt it.
I am broken and bored,
Is there any reward?
Reassure me, Good Lord,
And inform me about it,
Is there any reward?
I'm beginning to doubt it.

Do these poetic lines reflect the work of the homilist? No, they describe the doubts of a consistent consumer. Hilaire Belloc's context, larger than the confines of a church, is life itself. But if the formula proposed in the chapters above, namely, hard work and plenty of it, has any merit, there has to be some reward. There is and it is rich. The reward is absolutely correlative between homilists and those they serve. Indeed, it is not only correlative, it is reciprocal. The worshipers serve the homilists just as much as they are served by them.

THE COMMUNITY CREATED AND CREATING
The church is a worldwide community. This truth makes sense to the extent that there is also a local community, a corporate sense of the gathered faithful in each place where Christians assemble. "Oh, we're a congregation, all right, a

Sunday assembly, but we're not a community. You see, the people here in Zip Code 00000 don't. . . ." Don't what? They do assemble and they are the baptized. They look attentive, wherever their minds are; they respond to prayer and they sing; at the proper time they approach the Lord's table. What is there about them that makes a member, even a preacher, say that they are not a community?

There is an ancient dilemma with respect to the community: is it created or creating? On the one hand the eucharist with its homily (the sermon with its Lord's supper) creates community. Alternatively, though, without community there is nothing to celebrate. Both statements are true, of course, both ways of viewing the matter correct. However, a beginning must be made somewhere. Which comes first? Monastic communities say that a fitting celebration can only be made "around the altar and at the table." The meal is thought to give expression to fellowship as no formal worship can do. The Baptist coffee hour, the Methodist covered-dish supper, Catholic and Orthodox ethnic specialties of various kinds—all are the mortar that holds the stones of the gospel in place. Yet even food can be a contrived and empty symbol.

For a community to build and be built there has to be common purpose with respect to common concerns of the highest order. Where building needs to occur, whatever the failures of the past ("We've tried that," "It used to be better here before the new people moved in [the young people moved away]") effective preaching is a place to start. If the preaching stands apart from the total liturgy, however, it will also be the place to stop. "How did we manage to attract such a marvelous minister?" "That new priest is really something; even the ushers listen." All very fine as affirmation, as a subject of brief comment, but what does it mean for the long haul—for the community? How does it fit into the total work of proclaiming the gospel in the midst of this people? In what sense is the preaching worshipful and rewarding?

Interesting Preaching

First, the reward from the people's point of view. Most of them have been Christians for a long time, though some are recent converts and others new to the tradition of this particular church where they are now worshiping. Once they had great hopes for the gospel, though some have only lately come to know it as the force that is changing their lives. But whether they are long-time or new disciples, whether their heart-yearnings are a matter of years or only of months, they appear in the pews before us with the unspoken cry, "We long for the word. Feed us!"

Others here in the congregation are in a different condition. Restless at eight and glassy-eyed at twenty-eight, they have always done things in a conventional way. Churchgoing is one of the conventions. Every muscle in face and body conveys the apathy which says, "When will this be over?"

The congregants who hear our preaching are anything but homogeneous in their approaches to the homily. They are alike only in demanding that if there is to be pulpit talk it should be "interesting." They are not at all alike in the interest that qualifies the demand.

The Preached Word as Unifying Force

The homily is the irreplaceable opportunity to draw into unity all else that happens in the worship act. It does not "explain" the hymn or motet, or justify the music or dance. Least of all does it rationalize the ancient forms of address to God. What the homily does is draw together the disparate and elusive elements of a biblical word. It allows God to speak to an assembled people in a way that the circumstances of the sacred writings may impede. The summons to action in Christian worship is always biblical. God has many ways of addressing the community, chiefly the circumstances of their lives. But the experiences of the apostolic age are normative.

They are the founding events to which all subsequent ages must be related. People today cannot interpret what is happening to them in a context of faith if they know nothing of the experience of God of Moses and the prophets, if they do not recall to mind Jesus crucified and risen to the life of the new age. Exploring with them their attempts to make sense of their lives apart from the lives of their forerunners in faith may be an important service. It may even merit their gratitude. But it does not build their life in Christ. Only for the rejuvenating of this *life* have they come together. They are here to explore corporately who they are under the headship of Jesus their Lord, that they may give God the praise. To deal with them on any other terms is to trivialize their lives and trivialize the event.

God's biblical word to the people of God is not a book of oracles to be delivered with mantralike effect. The repetition of verbal material in familiar ways—the Jesus-prayer, the rosary, the litanies—has its place. But, biblical proclamation is of another order. There God addresses a people afresh through their ancestors in faith. As vessels of election these ancestors received an earlier deliverance. The hazards are evident. The biblical ages can be reconstructed falsely. The words of the books can be invested with a charmlike quality as if, having once been uttered, they achieve effect without relation to the life situation that brought them into existence. The biblical words must be proclaimed in faith if they are to be heard in faith. They cannot simply be reiterated orally as if the saying and the hearing accomplished anything in themselves. Once the faith proclamation is made, the biblical words must live with a life of their own in their hearers' hearts. For this the homily is not only helpful, it is indispensable.

Christians are one in space and time with all who have made the same faith-profession before them—especially those of the apostolic age. They are one with all their nameless coreligionists who make the same profession now. They are a worldwide, a cosmic company ("and so, with all the angels and archangels . . ."). Their primary community may be Old First Reformed or Augustana Lutheran or St. Aloysius, but the fellowship does not end there. It stretches out to every time and place. People need help in exercising their religious imagination to experience this unity. The strength of the homilist is especially needed. People can know themselves addressed by God if the voice of a prophet, a loving guide and teacher, speaks to them.

THE CALL TO LIFE

According to an old definition, a rut is a grave with the ends kicked out. More positively, biblical life and Christian life (they are one and the same) are ordinary life with its limits kicked out. Lives that are "cribb'd, cabin'd and confin'd" are destroyed by the power of the homilist's word, leaving "nothing but Christ in any of us."

The benefit of good preaching to worshipers is that for them it literally creates the church. It does this from week to week by making them conscious of their membership in the elect people. To be sure, they are faithful Presbyterians or Episcopalians or whatever it may be. They take this for granted, even as they take churchgoing for granted. But the power of the pulpit changes everything. It gives reasons for the prayer-act in *these* circumstances. It defines life as *purposeful* existence. To *be* is then to be *Christian* — to pray, decide, and act as followers of Jesus do. A pallid and predictable existence comes to an end. God speaks to the heart directly and immediately. The invitation, the summons requires an answer here and now.

Death-dealing Pulpits

No one is quite so desolate as the family or person who, having lived in the warmth of a community where the word of God was shared like a treasure, now must pray where a stone is offered for bread. Even more crushed than these, though, are the new Christians who have undergone conversion, who as adults have followed a course of instruction initiating them into a completely new life, who, a year or two after following the initial call receive the illumination of baptism — and then have to move. Even commoner perhaps is the disappointment of the person long estranged from earlier youthful allegiance as a Christian, who after years that may have been without meaning, experiences reconciliation in a communion with peculiarly attractive habits of prayer and then has to move to another town or state. Changes of location can mean both a change of pastors and the sickening reality of the empty pulpit. The homily that says nothing creates the suspicion that church life is, after all, just like ordinary life — all promise and no fulfillment. The worship assembly is a husk without a kernel, an empty rind. All the familiar ordinances of religion are there — the order of service, the music, the eucharist body of the Lord — but there is no realization of the body of Christ in human lives. From one week to the next the worship is worse than emptiness. It is a graveyard of dead forms.

Living with the Bible

The homily does not reward the worshipers immediately, like the administering of a dose of a much-needed prescription. The first reaction may be dismay. The preacher is leading the people into a biblical world in which they are not at home. This is no archaeological expedition but an induction into the life of the living church. Initially it may not be recognized as such. There may be the discomfort of unfamiliarity. Old and wellworn texts are being put to new uses; biblical tales are being unfolded that were never heard before. Above all, there is the rude shock of being told that this way alone is the way to a free and full life in Christ.

Nothing can be entirely welcome that reproaches what has gone before.

Biblical preaching, like Jesus' sword of division, separates those who wish to know more about the revealed word from those who find increasing reference to it a burden. From a keen minority there is bound to come a demand for Bible study. Preachers may be asked to have a part in this. If they accept it, it cannot be a controlled situation. The only control may be the direction that comes from the pulpit with regularity and serves as a basing point for all that is said in formal study. Far more important for fruitful preaching than formal study is individual Bible reading. Homilists must be prepared to share an intelligent schema for reading the Bible regularly. Without it their pulpit preaching will be sunsets for the blind and symphonies for the deaf.

Continuity in Preaching

It will not be long — a year, two years — before the preachers begin to hear from the assembly judgments and discernments based on the word preached. Interpretations, even random phrases, will be cited in their hearing and in their absence. At times we will be reminded of things months later we do not even remember having said. We will be challenged publicly in committee meetings on the basis of things we well remember having said. The supreme compliment comes when, like St. Paul, preachers have their own words cited against them. This proves that someone was listening, that at least one memorable statement was recorded.

Gradually, in all this, the assembly takes on the tone or character set by the preached word. A certain continuity and stability are required for this. The same worshipers must be led consistently by the same presider-preachers. With one pastor in a small church the problem is minimal — or maximal! Large congregations served by two or three who preach regularly cannot be assured of any outcome unless these ministers confer regularly about their task. Otherwise there is the painful situation of "catching the good one" — and this can make the last state of the congregation worse than the first.

The Energizing Word

The reward of an assembly in which the word is preached in and out of season is no less than Christian life itself. It is undisputable that the word of God makes the church be the church. The great sacramental symbols are essential here. Without them the Bible and its exposition can be a "head trip." Displays of unfeigned love and service are just as essential. A biblical and sacramental life is a symbolic life, symbolizing the mutual upbuilding and support of those who know how important they are to each other and to God. Effective preaching — defined as preaching that is *heard* — alone justifies costly educational structures and social services, appeals for support and public stands on moral questions. With it, a people knows why it is Christ in the world and hence wherefore it acts. Without it what remains is only a corps of sleepwalkers known as Christians — automatons with a label. They may think and organize and do, but there is no proper sense in which they *are*.

The energizing word creates and sustains a believing people. It makes those who say they are the body of Christ *be* the body of Christ. Without a word proclaimed the people perish — but, corpselike, keep coming to church.

LIFE FOR THE PREACHER

Effective preaching rewards homilists by giving meaning to our ministry. It situates us as persons in the church. Without it we are dislocated and lead false, often unhappy lives. With it our lives have the purpose we envisioned in youth. The endless round of duties and distractions that make up pastoral ministry is put in perspective as we

preachers begin to live in Christ ourselves and not just en-
courage others to do so. Like any believer, the preacher hopes
to live in a faith and love so complete that fear is cast out.
Clergy life is often fear-filled life, so strong a hold does the
prince of this world have on church people and institutions.
The demon can be cast out of oneself only as one casts it out
of others. Regular and intimate contact with the gospel does
this by identifying any cravenness as absurd. It indicates
where true power lies, showing that if God is not served in
love the awesome Majesty alone is to be feared. All human
and demonic powers are reduced to nothingness in face of
this sovereign and majestic Love. To summon others to full
life in Christ is to hear the call oneself. Answering it is easier
if one goes forward in the company of congregants who
become friends.

The Personal Benefits

Let us attempt in the simplest fashion a list of benefits to
the preacher (with it our presentation will be over):

• Preparation for preaching requires study. It makes
homilists lifetime students of the scriptures, which is the
reason we pursued a theological education in the first place.

• Preaching effectively stimulates a love of language. It
discourages the debasement of words by those called to speak
God's word in words.

• Preparing homilies that move the hearer entails the lost
art of argument. With fuzziness exorcised from the homilist's
mind, thought processes prosper.

• Attempting to preach well makes us preachers face our
prejudices and preconceptions. Christian convictions are a
blessing. Without them no one could preach. But the search
for persuasive discourse requires the marshalling of pros and
cons, and opposing positions are seen for the first time in all
their attractiveness.

• Preaching keeps one humble. Persistence at it sends one's

standards higher. In preaching we accomplish what we set out to do no more than half the time.

• Reaching the hearers (probably on the "failure" days by the homilist's standard) begets appreciation. We need to know that we are useful, and the signals come. The word of affirmation from an unexpected source—subtract all those generous sentiments at the church door—can keep us going for a year.

• Most important, preaching faithfully has a way of bringing all of life into focus for the preacher. When one has one's first real insights as to what it means to be a disciple it is time to die or retire—not altogether a bad thing.

The Challenge

Let us try to sum up.

Life in the ministry is full of discouragements. Preaching is its balm. Life for the faithful, just plain life for people generally, is largely discouragement. Preaching is its balm. Preaching can also be an irritant to the hearer—and the more evangelical the preaching the more irritating it is—but without a grain of sand no oyster ever makes a pearl.

What if preaching, though, is the chief irritant in the *preacher's* life, as it often is? The truth here is that one has to become minimally good at giving a homily before it yields any satisfaction. Weekly humiliation may be the stuff of self-oblation, but it is not a good formula for service. Like anything human—a talent for parenting, a coordinated golf swing, conversing at one's ease—delivering a homily must be done at the minimum level of self-confidence that provides enjoyment. Joy to the preacher is joy to the people. Misery to the assembly is misery to the preacher (should that worthy be listening). Jesus was not very comfortable on his cross but, for the rest, you can be sure he liked his work. He was good at it.

Our medieval forebears described our sin-stained world as "a vale of tears." God made our world and it is good—but there is a serpent in the garden. Our rebelliousness casts a pall over all. The preaching of the gospel, however, brings joy to the world, not mindless delight but the secure conviction that God in Christ has overcome the world. The preacher is the herald of this joy.

The times we live in are a strange mixture of great wealth and great poverty, maximum possessions for some and minimum peace for most. The churches are convinced of their message, God's truth. Many people, though, have left the churches to pursue hucksters of salvation. Many, too, have left the churches of their youth to follow purveyors of a different salvation: TM, est, venture capital, healthful living. The church continues to be where it was. It will always be present where the gospel is preached. As to those assemblies where it is not preached, in what sense are they any longer the church?

Honest reporting from lands abroad reveals a horrifying picture of regimes and armies that are busy at the calculated destruction of their own populations. Can there be priests and ministers among us who are no less destructive of the faith of our people? Not consciously, certainly, but none the less truly.

Disedifying conduct can take its toll on the church's life, as can harsh treatment of congregation members or comfortable living in the midst of poverty. All these matters are as nothing, however, compared to the open wound in the side of Christ which is bad preaching, preaching that proclaims — nothing. Words, words, words.

Those of us who are empowered to proclaim God's word today have the power to make it a revolutionary force. We can have a part in the birth of faith, in re-creating the church. We can help to save the world. My God, what a life!

68419